Encouragement Hope Divine Dialogue

A Collection

AuthorHouse™
1663 Liberty Drive
Bloomington, IN 47403
www.authorhouse.com
Phone: 1 (800) 839-8640

Scripture quotations marked NIV are taken from the Holy Bible, New International Version®. NIV®. Copyright © 1973, 1978, 1984 by International Bible Society. Used by permission of Zondervan. All rights reserved. [Biblica]

Published by AuthorHouse 03/06/2019

ISBN: 978-1-5462-6880-2 (sc)
ISBN: 978-1-5462-6879-6 (e)

Library of Congress Control Number: 2018913637

Print information available on the last page.

This book is printed on acid-free paper.

author**HOUSE**®

Encouragement

Acknowledgements

My deepest thanks to Lisa McGowan of ColorByNumberDesign for all her assistance, and kindness, in bringing this book to fruition. This is a debt of gratitude that can never be repaid.

Kudos to Natalie Dumanian also from CBN, for her remarkable design sense. Infinite thanks too, to my loving wife Frances, for her infinite patience and help in this labor of love.

Heartfelt thanks also to Authorhouse, and particularly to Karen Adamson, whose infinite patience I dearly hope will be in some small way rewarded with these inadequate words.

I'd like also to take a moment to personally acknowledge the people of our local coffeehouses - the staff, the characters, the youth on parade, the denizens, and the families - those who often make up the best part of our day.

Here is a place to be out in the marketplace, yet conduct our private tasks (such as the compiling and editing of this book). Here is a place to gather the smile that makes a better day, to give a nod or share a word about life. Thanks to Anne, to Meagan, to Rob, to Barbie, and Steve, and John. Thanks for the simple inquiries on the healing of a broken toe; thanks for the sturdy voice of our local contrarian; the stock tips from our retired broker; thanks for the mathematical visions of our local Laureate

Here perhaps is the only "community" - outside our insular households - many of us will know.

Thanks to all. Surely, God willing, I will see you all again, tomorrow.

The Author

Welcome

Stir your soul,
along with me
with thoughts of the infinite;
that this morning's light
may be tinted with
the hues of grace
and the wonders of this season,
as we walk
on these pathways to the infinite.

Into a Boundless Reality

I feel my heart beating,
it says I'm alive.
This gentle resolute pounding
one two three four five,
Pushing my life's blood
vitality
through each and every vein,
the vigor of endless ages in me.
And how do we capture
the passion and commitment
of Divinity?
How reach down into a
boundless reality
so far beyond the knowledge
of so shallow an instrument
as this conscious brain.

Sweet divine reality
beyond our ken
If you must needs hint only
hint away.
If you must refuse to shout
I will learn to listen
more intently
to the silence
which bears your mark,
And I will check my pulse
to gauge the quiet trampings
of your good tread.

This new life has gained its sturdy foothold within.

That little sprout, standing alone,
at the cusp of light and shadow
This new life
new perspective
has gained its sturdy foothold
within
Claims its patch of warm earth
striving up
Reaching blind yet unerringly
for the light which sustains
its most energetic soul.

Vibrant life
full of promise
rooted beneath the
chill evidence of
yesterday's storm
Striving irresistibly upward
into today's light
and tomorrow's.

Deep notes,
breeze notes,
the natural hum
of the earth in
rotation.

In each of us
there are such awesome potentials,
such grandeurs,
hope ever rekindling.

Let that light ever burn in me,
as at this moment.
Fresh as morning, filled with
the breeze of the morrow
which so often billows our sails
till the spars creak,
the canvas-weave
stretches fine,
and the lines are so taught
as to sing in the wind.
Deep notes, breeze notes,
the natural hum
of the earth in rotation,
while the moon tugs
and dances in its arms.
A loving universal dance
all expressed
in this one breeze
one boat
one set of sail.

Put faith before you as the
end to which you devote
all your means.

It will come
when most needed and will be
your constant companion.

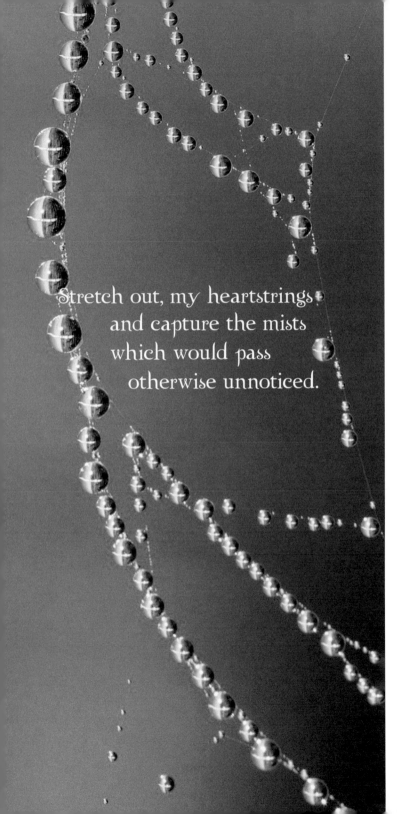

Stretch out, my heartstrings
and capture the mists
which would pass
otherwise unnoticed.

Stretch out! Stretch out!
my heartstrings.
Like the silken cross-weave
of spiders' web
catching the morning dew,
in its turn to catch
the golden glorious morning light.

Stretch out! Stretch out!
and let the wet settle
on this weave,
till each new drop, heavy
with the accumulated contribution
of each misty droplet,
stretches itself,
magnifying its own small frame
of the distant perspective
in a gleaming fleeting
yearning grasp towards the earth
Then falling, round again,
to meet its appointed place
on this earth.

Stretch out, my heartstrings
and capture the mists
which would pass
otherwise unnoticed
and uneventful,
Never to gather or share
in meaning.
gather the mists of this life
in unique reunion.

I choose rather
to remember
the wind-swept curls
with sun's halo,
the laughing eyes.

One child
full of laughter,
with smiling eyes,
joins you in the sun
and salty breeze
at the edge
of the surging tide,
To playfully contribute
to your sand-castle
her own sea-shells
sea-weed pods
and tufts of heather,
Then laughing, runs away.

This I will remember and take heart

While another
with more resonant laugh
comes stomping
brutish
in the midst of
your lovingly-built world
To stand astride its ruin
defiant
beefy fists
cockily planted on hips
green-giant-like
But jolly not.

How easy
to remember the ruin
the double salted tears
spiced
with wind-borne salt spray
stinging.
How easy to remember
that passion
in destruction.

But I choose rather
to remember
the wind-swept curls
with sun's halo
the laughing eyes,
that last touch
of yellow-flowered heather
placed lovingly
on the parapets.

How light her step
tread of an angel
as she dancingly retreated
at the fringes
of white-foamed
whispering surf.

So soon her dimpled footprints
disappeared
as each wave after wave
did its work to erase
her passing.
Transforming her footsteps
back to native washed sand
each grain carried, even now,
closer to that equatorial realm
which is the destination
of all the tides.

This I will remember
and take heart.
This I will remember
and rejoice.

You can do all things
and you will.

Your hands are strong
and your heart beats excitedly
with the knowledge
that you can do all things
and you will.
You are smart and capable
filled with the abundance
of new things.

Your hands can form
new worlds
and can also work
in the least of things
to bring about changes
for the good
for the betterment of others.
I will support you in this.
My Spirit will guide
and my strength will provide.

Your hands can form
new worlds
and can also work
in the least of things.

There is a song
within you
which will yet
be sung.
Be assured of it.

When the Spirit of life
is awakened in you
the light of that Spirit
will become a
sparkling light
reflected across
the waters
after the day has set
into night.

I promise you
the light
grows ever brighter
as we rush to
meet you,
in a splash of light
and laughter
sweet consolation.
Light and laughter,
the sun and wind
bright clouds of white
in the bluest of skies
wet with love
and a heart alive
for you.

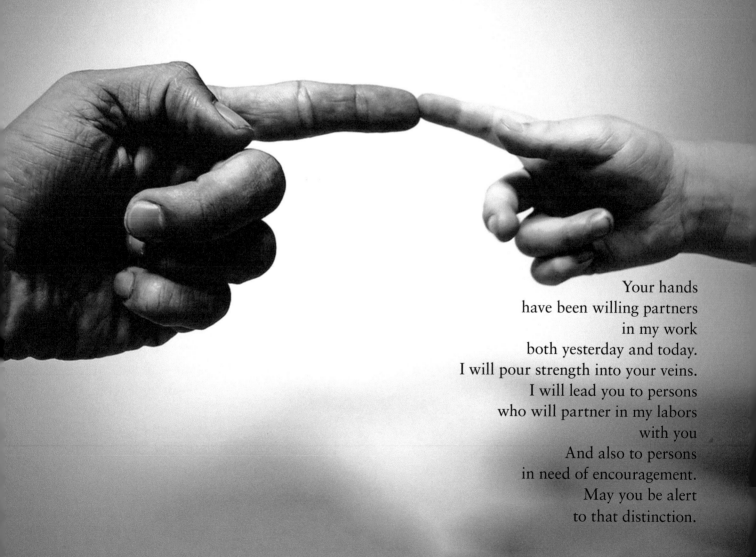

I will pour strength
into your veins.

Your hands
have been willing partners
in my work
both yesterday and today.
I will pour strength into your veins.
I will lead you to persons
who will partner in my labors
with you
And also to persons
in need of encouragement.
May you be alert
to that distinction.

Reveal the far horizons
within me now.

Lord that I might find
the heart of perfect silence
within me now.
Lord that stillness
might reign supreme
in my mind
a perfect setting
for paradise,
a perfect setting
for the gem of your presence.
Father reveal the far horizons
within me now.

Liquid substance of
Happiness
flows from my heart.

Today a joy
has overtaken my heart
inexplicably
And it seems
I have only to press
some inner
ventricular button
And liquid substance of
Happiness
flows from my heart.

Your light shines brighter still.
Each day is brighter still,
till the full light of day.
Let your feet run to do good,
and your path be right.
Hear the voice within you
saying "Walk this way."

Here is a voice you can trust.
Only seek it
discern it
capture it
nurture and foster it
amplify it
and tune to it always.
This voice will be your guide
and encouragement.
This voice will lead you
in the way everlasting.

Hear the voice within you
saying "Walk this way".
Here is a voice you can trust.

How full of life
just outside my window.
How full is life
just inside my heart.

I have walked through raindrops
felt the chill wet on my toes
and it seems somehow grand
and simple.

The strings of your heart
are tuned
to a perfect pitch.

So much trial in a life
can take its toll.
You can rest in the knowledge
that the strings of your heart
are tuned to a perfect pitch
always at the ready
to ring true.
Make a habit of this
and you will find satisfaction
unlimited
through all your days.

19

My soul is at peace
and life is good.

I let go the reins of my soul
and allow my soul
to have its head
To take me where it will
as the goodness of God
will lead.
My soul is at peace
and life is good
this moment at least.
Uncomplicated
and unfettered.

The music of heaven,
filled with ideals
and noble sentiments

The music of your activities
is the music of heaven,
filled with ideals
and noble sentiments.

Were all humanity to collaborate
according to our ideals
would not this world
see singing
and hear the bird's song.

The song is in the trees
though the storm's approaching.
The light is in the leaves
even when the rain is pouring.

I would that each day
could bring such peace.
I would that every activity
could bring such reward.

The firework. display
of another thought
just a thought
sets my heart to racing
with love, or fear, or joy
and the most treasured,
precious memory
of a sister, a niece,
a big-hearted
brother-in-law
and a tear trickles
from my eye
in gratitude.
Effortless,
the winds of my soul
driving the sails
in this pleasure-dome
picture-play.

A heartbeat away
from eternity,
the march of times
through a life
bound only by
the integrity of I,
and I alone to bind it.

Just a thought
sets my heart
to racing
with love.

There is joy in
the plaintive
bird-song and echo
of childish laughter
in another gentle soul.

There is joy in the freedom
to listen with intent
and hear
the plaintive
bird -song and echo
of childish laughter
in the modest
daily discourse
of another gentle soul.

How ennobling
to feel the heart beating
in step
with the fulsome
ebb and flow
of our neighbor's
ever-slighted commentary.

I will enrich
and bathe myself in it.
I will abandon
my own trajectory
if only for a moment
to feel the pulse
and heartbeat inherent
in the noble souls
who commit their time
to pass the time merely
and I will cherish it.

We have begun
our opus.
Now it begins.

The lyre is prepared
and the harp is tuned,
The brass polished
to a fine gleam.
And as the sun rises,
there is a spirit in the air
alive with you
and alive with so many.

The first notes are struck
and swelling anticipation
in my own heart
is felt in the hearts of all.

The first notes are struck;
the strings, and the brass,
and the reeds are ready.

About These Writings

Before establishing a peaceful home on
Long Island, the author's burdens
and anguished memory would come to
form a seemingly insurmountable barrier
to happiness.

So, pen in hand, he began the search for that inner
voice of divine hope and encouragement within. A
small fraction of the results can be found on these
pages.

If these words resonate for you, it is only because this
is the same voice that stirs within you, attuned to a
perfect harmonious pitch with all your neighbors.

A note on reading these texts:

These writings are often in Call-and-Response form.
You will hear a needy heart, then a second voice of
encouragement and strength. This second voice is generally
shown following the photo-icon of a dandelion, as on page 34.
It is hoped that you may find the encouragement you may need
at times as well.

Hear
the voice of angels
in the sea.

How can can I thank you Lord
for delivery from all forms
of anguish and frustration
to leave my heart perfect still
and able to hear
the voice of angels
in the sea,
and to delight in the sound
of foam
in a shell.

Divine Dialogue

Finding Divine Encouragement in a 21st Century World

Dipped in Liquid Light

That Invisible Thread

The Crickets' Calls

Canvas the Blessings

This Voice

A Child with a Plaything

Ventricular Button

It Seems Somehow Grand

Forgiveness of Folly

A Rainbow's Heart

A Plaything in Joy

Sweet Consolation

A Moment Poised Between Rest and Labor

Introduction

"In every winter's heart there is a quivering spring, and behind
the veil of each night there is a smiling dawn."
—Gibran

Hope, as defined, must know the depths to gain the sense that there will be something better. From anguish is born release, and through release, joy. Anguish is heavy, pregnant with release. The vision of, the sense of, that release we all have known, because the blackest of despair cannot remain. It is always overthrown. This too is inevitable. The least of things – a scent, a kind word, a letter of gratitude, unbinds that force within us, and catches us quite by surprise. We call it "Hope."

These writings are for the most part born of suffering, drawn up from a deep well of morning. Where joy is expressed, it is only found and recognized as a breakthrough from despair. That breakthrough emotion, for me, happens when, pen in hand, a voice of the divine encouragement emerges.

Provider, lover, encourager, friend a solace in trouble and a plaything in joy.

Sweet consolation, the spirit divine never directs. The spirit's voice transforms our view of the kingdom, like a window onto a garden, with spring in full bloom, accompanied by the trill of bird-song. It reminds us of something deep within-only dimly perceived, half-forgotten, on the fringes of memory – our native home, our heavenly habitation.

Choose Hope. Above all else, write of Hope, and she will catch you unawares, like morning light, cascading inevitably across the eastern windowsill, through no effort of your own.

The light has yet to arrive
from that orb
You have ordained
to rise each day.
I light a few candles
for a softening glow
across the pages
as the ink does its work
carrying what is inside, out.

Dipped in Liquid Light

It is morning, before the dawn
and my heart goes out
to you Lord.
The light has yet to arrive
from that orb
You have ordained
to rise each day.
I light a few candles
for a softening glow
across the pages
as the ink does its work
carrying what is inside, out.

My heart, you are softened today.
The quiet is welcome
Outside and in.
Yearnings, for this moment
are held at bay
And I gaze inside
at a horizon of peace.
I have seen the moon
at its full
bright through
the silhouetted branches
and leaves of the evening trees
And this has been pleasant
to my soul.

I have seen the herons
Both in the sparkling light
of morning
at the bay
as the gulls laughed
And in the evening rosy glow
of setting day.
They stand erect so patiently
legs dipped in liquid light
awaiting a meal
to come swimming by
as it will
When their head, and that curve of neck
dashes forward
faster than perception
to gather in the harvest.

Lord give me that patience
give me that surety
grant me that life
standing in liquid light
certain of my daily bread
While the sun makes its rounds
from morning till night.

9/30/07
Stony Brook

Lord give me that patience
give me that surety
grant me that life
standing in liquid light
certain of my daily bread
While the sun makes its rounds
from morning till night.

A Rainbow's Heart

How sweet and glorious
how wonderful to find You
to know Your presence
to take time for hearing Your voice.
Great are you Lord
to fill my heart.
Great is the mercy, the grace and the power
that can give to my heart
this greatest of gifts.
An hour in your word
when the switch in my heart
is switched on to you
is worth a thousand of diversions.

It feels like life
like the sun is kind
and the air is sweet
and beneath the noise
is a rainbow's heart.
Sing Lord sing.
let your voice be heard.

My child, your heart
as many a heart
has been sorely tried these days.
Your body has been bruised
by the cacophony of noise
and the poking, the prodding
of a hundred aggressive fingers
Prompting you onward
in a hundred directions
while all the while
you know not where you go.

There is nothing to do, but this:
to find shelter in my word
to draw into my place
within you.
Let the world go by
a moment only.
It will pass alone
without your prompting.
Your business is to know me
to call on me
and sing.

Take my word and let it ring
within your soul
to captivate your heart.
Let the song of ages ring
the psalm of a generation be sung.
There is more to this business
of achieving my presence

than you can know
Yet you cannot know it
it will know you.
In simplicity is your strength
confirmed only by your inner senses.
Your faith returns day by day;
Faith of the fathers
holy faith
A faith that will be with you
till death.
Faith above all
the strength of a God
who overcomes all,
Strength of a God
who fills you now.

9/24/07
Stony Brook

It feels like life
Like the sun is kind
and the air is sweet
And beneath the noise
is a rainbow's heart.

A Child with a Plaything

My God, how unsettled my heart
and filled with trouble.
Could more "what if's" and
"if only's" be found
surely I would unearth them
and toy with them,
like a child with a plaything.
Grant that I might get up and over this stage.
Grant that I might overcome.
Surely many are the days
when the light seems bright.
Surely there will be nights of peace
and deep satisfaction.
Yet for now I am blind
to anything
save this bloody discomfort
this nagging uneaqse.

Lord, overcome this within me
or direct me to that prayer
or action which dispels
like smoke before a fan.

My son, comfort is the real illusion
and the bane of a righteous life.
To know only comfort is to know no growth.
Grow now, in this new soil.
Spread your roots,
draw nourishment up
from the soil about you.
Drink deep, then spread your branches
to the light.
Soak up the goodly rays
of heavenly sun.
Within you is the key to heaven.
Open always is the door.
Step in and sing.

Stony Brook
7/10/06

Drink deep, then spread
your branches to the light.
Soak up the goodly rays
of heavenly sun.
Within you is the key to heaven.

A Plaything in Joy

Lord, nothing is more important
than my wife's happiness.
Let me be the kind of loving companion
she would desire.
Let me become
all that you have designed me to be.
Provider, lover, encourager, friend
a solace in trouble
and a plaything in joy.

You have so much to give
a sensitive heart
a delicate conscience
a strong mind
and a flexible will.
You turn your intelligence
to the task of making a home
and providing for shelter.
You provide the livelihood that is your share
and you take the role
defined by tradition

yet tempered by the comforts
of contemporary thought.
You provide respect and consideration.
You give of your time as generously
as is possible
and your thoughts are kind.

Stony Brook
2007

Tomorrow lies at the horizon
and while the curve of this earth
may hide the path
beyond that next bend

Yet you know that path leads on
to a heavenly realm
and many a pilgrim
has trod this way before you.

A Moment Poised Between Rest and Labor

Jesus, it is morning
and your hand is upon me once again.
The snow blankets all things
and I am poised between rest and labor.
Quietly, softly, music, a piano, loving singer
sings of love
And my loving wife lies quietly, softly
taking a few more well deserved
moments of rest.
Soon, very soon, she will rise
and give her energies
her love in motion
in a most natural and instinctive drive
to give of herself,
and the love that springs unerringly,
unfailingly
from her heart.
How sweet, delicious, these precious moments
set apart, a world apart
from the roadways
and ledgers,
the press of diverse
and so often divisive

ambitions.
Sweetly, sweetly, these moments pass
and I know that demands will come,
Your commands to live fully
will win over this invisible desire
to return to sweet dreams.
I will apply my hands to so many endeavors
in search of destiny
that unending search for destiny.
Jesus, it is morning
the slightest chill
remains in the air
and invades my robe,
pleasantly – this is life.
Joy comes to my heart
and a tear to my eye
in gratitude.
So fleeting, these tender emotions
you have built into our frame
I desire most profoundly to hold it,
in both hands
and never let go.

My wife, dear wife, comes to me
quietly, gently

with a pot of warm mint tea
Already she responds to that
unerring need within
to give of her love
and the tears roll one after the other
down my cheek
in tender gratitude.

Gently love-songs rise
from the stereo.
The tea is warm
and the mint reminds me
of springtime gardens
in family life so long ago
While my wife, in a few words
alludes of Christmas
a few words only
yet so deeply reassuring.
And my heart returns to gratitude.
I know these gentle moments will pass
quickly, so quickly.
The insistence of life
will replace
the persistence of dreams.

I hear the cars on the road in the distance
yet my desire for quiet remains.
So few are these days
These opportunities to speak with You again
unreservedly
As one, to the One
who is the source

of all my health
both without and within.
Lord accept my words
may You take some pleasure
in my gratitude
and in my reflections on You.
Soon, so soon, I will go
and the demands of this day
in upsets and uncertainties
will remind me
of yesterday's upsets and emergencies.
Soon, but not yet.
In a few words my wife
seeks assurance
I have enough light
for this my labor of love.
And my heart again is reassured
by her unfailing concern
driven by a love
that emerges from
some eternal wellspring
deep within her soul.
How can I end these moments?
The morning sun slants low
through the window
brightly lighting
the pinks and whites
of the clustered flowers
on the potted Cyclamen
on the table just before me.
The sun, the light, has come to me
through no effort of my own

and the shadows in the pinks and whites
take definition.

Can this be? The light has passed on?
It falls in a slanted beam now
across my page
works now across the room
to where sits my wife
sharing with me
these love-songs.
But no, the light returns fully
to the flowers just before my eyes
and I am reassured
this day
will not pass that quickly.
A cloud or two will pass
and the light will return, brightly.
The light finds me
through no effort of my own
And my wife comes to me
to place a warm and caring hand
across my chest.
The warmth that emanates
from that little hand
is always so great a surprise.
With a few words, she moves away
and again the tears trickle down.
There is love indeed in her heart.
There is love in the labors of these
gifted singers
Jim Brickman, Michael W. Smith
And all this comes to me

through no effort of my own.
How can we earn such moments?
Could we package it please
then pass it along to those
in need of shelter.
So many, right now,
in despair and appall
so recent too,
my own despairing and appall.
Recharge my fuel cells with this my Love
Let me ever carry the knowledge that these
moments always return
No matter how far we may wander
in our endless pursuits for Something.
These moments can sustain a multitude of days:
A shout triumphant, in a moment silent.

The light falls soft on my hand and my pen.
The light comes soft
to my heart and my soul.
Sing in me, song of ages
and let this song be heard by all
In a moment fleeting,
with my eternal companions
In a moment poised between
rest and labor.
My God to you I owe all this
and more.

Amen
Stony Brook, NY
2/12/06

I know these gentle moments will pass
quickly, so quickly.
The insistence of life
will replace
the persistence of dreams

These moments can sustain
a multitude of days.
A shout triumphant, in
a moment silent.

My Heart Today

My heart is broken today
and all the pillows
and teddy bears
and blankets
of the guest room
Cannot bring me to my senses.
I am filled with a longing
for a fullness of You.
The sharp edges of this world
cut like shards of glass
on my consciousness.
I seek some means
to soften the edges
That my thoughts might be
sweet to me
sweet to You.

There are delicate flowers
and elephant-ear leaves
under radiant rosy
late-afternoon light
to be called up
from the treasure chest of memory.
There are images of
diamond-strewn harbors
brushed by the cool breezes
at end of day.
Yet I choose

the losses
that make me bleed.

Enough!
I will have
more of beauty
and less of the beastly.
I will call up heaven
though hell's gates
open wide
calling.

My God, entice me
with the sweet cooling love-songs
that bless the angels' hearts
and fill their wings
to make them fly.
And I will fly.
I will fly to Your presence
fill my wings
with Your spirit.
I will take
the vision of heaven
glimmering just below
the horizons of perception
and let it arise glowing
into a glorious morning dawn
filled with promise.

Arise my soul
take wing.
The thermals of the air this day
are perfect for flight
and heaven calls.
I leave the weight on my feet
and feel the wind on my wings.
The soaring of our flock
can be seen to the far horizons.
We are wind-borne and heaven-bound.
The crimson-tinged dawn
arises beyond that next
snow-bound peak
and we are borne to the east
on an westerly wind.

When we arrive
as we will
at that rainbow's end
that treasure will not be buried

but will fill our hearts
to bursting
and fill our eyes
with tears.
The gladness of reunion
At heaven's door
with our maker
our mothers and fathers
Sisters and brothers
alive together
in the whiteness
and softness of clouds
Full of harmony.
Let us sing
a song of reunion.
Our hearts are free.

Stony Brook
6/30/2008

Let us sing
a song of reunion.
Our hearts are free.

There are delicate flowers
and elephant-ear leaves
under radiant rosy
late-afternoon light
to be called up
From the treasure chest
of memory.

The soaring of our flock
can be seen to the far horizons.
We are wind-borne
and heaven-bound.

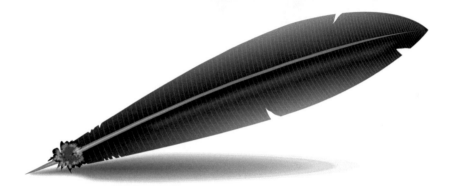

Take a large scroll
and write on it
with an ordinary pen...

Is 8:1

My heart is stirred
by a noble theme
as I recite my verses
for the king;
My tongue is the pen
of a skillful writer.

Ps 45:1

Writing...

We grow up with writing as a task.

Given our ABCs we dutifully practice:
*   between the lines*
*   upper case*
*   lower case.*

Next we are given a book report to write. Diligently we read, then invent some string of words we hope will please "...the author is making a metaphor to..." Yet what we feel as we write might be, that the day is so fine, we'd like to be out with our friends, or joining brother Ed for that program we so want to see.

Again your parents might remind you that a thank-you note is necessary. So obediently we write - yet our heart is far from a heartfelt "...Thank You..."

Then at work, we must deliver a report. So while our heart is dreaming of the next vacation, tonight's outing, new companion, old friend; or struggling with our latest office faux pax, our heart is out there, while professionally we write "... costs of the project were above forecasts due to unforeseen ..."

Our heart is one place, and our pen in another.

So by rote and repetitive practice, the act of writing becomes an errand, a chore to accomplish. Writing is decidedly detached from the heart. Even while journaling we write a chronicle "...we did this, I did that..." while our passions wander elsewhere. We lose the true purpose and charm of writing – to COMMUNICATE. The left brain writes, and the right brain emotes, in separate hemispheres, worlds apart.

But this is like running with your thumbs in your pockets. There is no real momentum with the swing of the torso disengaged; the passions hang limp at your side. But read the Psalms of David and you will discover another form. All of the joys and anguish; tears and swelling pride, are revealed at the nib of the writing pen.

The writings in DIVINE DIALOGUES were borne on days of deep anxiety:
> "So many long hours of labor
> yet today I am not comforted
> and melancholy descends
> once again."

But the seeds of transition are planted in the writing, and soon grow unerringly:
> "The song is in the trees
> though the storm's approaching.
> How full of life
> just outside my window.
> How full is life
> just inside my heart."

The pen is a mighty tonic, and you can take your fill without prescription. It is available anytime you can steal away a few moments. Most importantly it is available when the chaos of living and the alternatives of the future create only an inner miasma of mind, with no pathway out.

This is writing, giving all your feeling, all your sentimentalism, releasing all your passion, letting it all out, self-expression. And the reward is a gentle stilling of the heart, a release, an afterglow.

When the burden is too great, lay it down, lift it up, whatsoever feels of release.
You can do this, and better.
You can gain this reward, and more.

Long Valley, NJ
7/4/2008

You are a spring enclosed, a sealed fountain…

SS 4:12

Awake, north wind,
and come south wind!
Blow on my garden,
that its fragrance may spread abroad.

SS 4:16

Canvas the Blessings

Lord this day opened up like a delicate flower
sensitive, lightly unfurling
to the light of morning.
My heart is at peace, and my mind gentles me
with thoughts of those
who give of themselves
with liberality.
Take this day and shine in it, in me.
All that has been lost, is my gain in you.
Let the windows in my heart
look out at the dawn
across the lattice of my neighbor's yard
into the flowering of spring
on the hedges beyond.

Canvas the blessings of this life
and you will find
many a good thing in your past
Worthy of reflection
and gratitude,
At every turn, a sheltering hand
a word of encouragement
an enlightening thought,
At every corner, a directing hand
pointing the way:
"This is the way, walk in it."

Stony Brook
2007

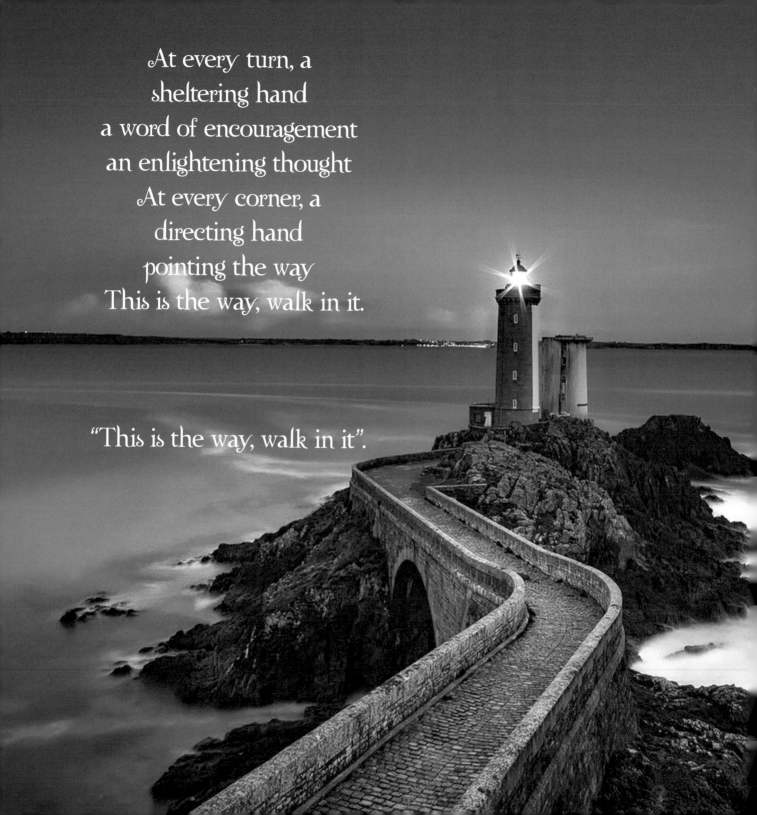

At every turn, a
sheltering hand
a word of encouragement
an enlightening thought
At every corner, a
directing hand
pointing the way
This is the way, walk in it.

"This is the way, walk in it".

Forgiveness of Folly

Bless you Lord
for you have changed
my crying to laughter.
My soul is singing in my breast
a song of ages, and of generations past.
There is no fear for now
for safety
for provision
for turmoil and drama.
There is only hope
and the knowledge
that we have done right in your eyes
because our flaws are covered
with a robe of perfection
the robe of Christ
for the forgiveness of folly.

Your hands are strong
and your heart beats excitedly
with the knowledge
that you can do all things
and you then will.
You are smart and capable
filled with the abundance
of new things.
Your hands can form
new worlds
And can also work
in the least of things
to bring about changes for the good
for the betterment of man.
I will support you in this.
My Spirit will guide
and my strength will provide.

Stony Brook
2007

My soul is singing
in my breast
a song of ages,
and of generations past.
There is no fear for now
for safety
for provision
for turmoil and drama.
There is only hope.

Sweet Consolation

My child, bring your heart to me.
This is our anguish.
I will share this with you awhile.
Let me confide in you now
that this pain will rend our frame
only this little while.
I promise you sweet moments
of laughter
so deep you have not known it
since early days of childhood
When the knowledge of good and evil
existed only as a lesson
taught by parents
in a book that remained
on the highest shelf.
There is a song within you
which will yet be sung.
Be assured of it.
When the Spirit of life
is awakened in you
The light of that Spirit
will become a sparkling light
reflected across the waters
after the day has set
into night.

I promise you the light
grows ever brighter
as we rush to meet you.
We will meet in a splash of light
and laughter
sweet consolation.
Light and laughter, the sun and wind
Bright clouds of white
in the bluest of skies
Wet with love and a heart alive
for you.

7/11/90

A perfect setting
for paradise
a perfect setting
for the gem
of your presence.

That Invisible Thread

Lord that I might find
the heart of perfect silence
within me now.
Lord that stillness
might reign supreme
in my mind
a perfect setting
for paradise
a perfect setting
for the Gem of your presence.
Father reveal the far horizons
within me now.
How secure is that invisible thread
from me to You
And how sweet the tie that binds.
I look and do not see
but rather feel
and the sense of You
brings comfort to the heart
Yet still I look
for your face
for your smile
for your word
for the butterfly-wings
of your presence
in the stillness within.

Let the clatter of this world recede
till all I see
is the silken thread
full of light
and touched with the dew of heaven
that leads to you.

My son, your hands
have been willing partners
in my work
both yesterday and today.
I will pour strength into your veins.
I will lead you to persons
who will partner in my labors
with you
And also to persons
in need of encouragement.
May you be alert
to that distinction.

Into your heart now
I give my Spirit.
The waters of heaven flow
within your veins.
And while your Humanity
will often emerge
So too will your Heavenly.
The water and the blood
of my Son's heritage
Flows even now
in your veins
If you ever return to me
I will ever return to you
To reassure you ever
that this is so.
Can you not feel the strength of your heart?
The years yet bound
within the flex
of this hearty flesh.

This ground is being softened again
that it might be fertile soil
for the planting of my word.
Do you not feel
the years yet to be?
the strength in potential?
Tomorrow lies at the horizon
and while the curve of this earth
may hide the path
beyond that next bend
Yet you know that path leads on
to a heavenly realm
And many a pilgrim has trod
this way before you.
Take comfort now
and sing within your soul
along with me.

7/27/06
Stony Brook

We will meet in a
splash of light
and laughter
sweet consolation.
Light and laughter,
the sun and wind
Bright clouds of white
in the bluest of skies
Wet with love and
a heart alive
for you.

The Crickets' Calls

The crickets' calls
abuzz in all the trees about me
this early morning
And the occasional bird lifts its voice
to the growing light.
Somehow the crickets are always
a background sound
until you turn your attention to them.
Then it rises and falls, breaks and chirps
comes close, then recedes.
How many of their kind do I hear now?
Countless, unimaginable.
For when I leave to drive
from here to fifty miles from here
still a whirring steady buzz
is heard through the open window
above the roll of the tires
and the rush of wind past my ear.
So may the voice and will of God
be to me
Steady, unceasing,
always there
when I turn
my attention to it.
So may the sense of God's presence
eternal, and stretching out
beyond all my horizons be.

My child you have
wood for the fire
light enough for every room
Food enough
to entertain
a family of ten
The light I give this morning
you are assured
will last till evening.
The trees will grow
the leaves will turn
to brilliant autumn glow
In the suns of autumn
while the evergreen needles
hold their green
hold their ground
against the coming onslaught
of winter
All this life
of birds and bugs
will survive
most nobly
full of energy
the spirit of life.

So is your heart.
it will change, in part
most profoundly
with the changing of the light
and the times of day.
Then too it will remain
in part
evergreen
to hold its own
against any chill
it may encounter
in its coming days
When your heart has been tried
once again
by the season's turning.
Spring once again
will begin its inevitable march
across this planet
To warm a heart turned bitter cold
under the icy blast.

The leaves will green once again
with the lengthening days.
The sheltering canopy overhead
will be spread
to cool now
and shade
against the excesses
of the sun

So is my provision.
It goes around
and comes round again
Season after season.
With trust and faith
you can trust in my return
rest in my growth within
as a sheltering canopy
an evergreen guarantee
an endless voice
rising and falling in your attention
Yesterday was, and tomorrow will be
But now is all in all.

10/7/07
Stony Brook

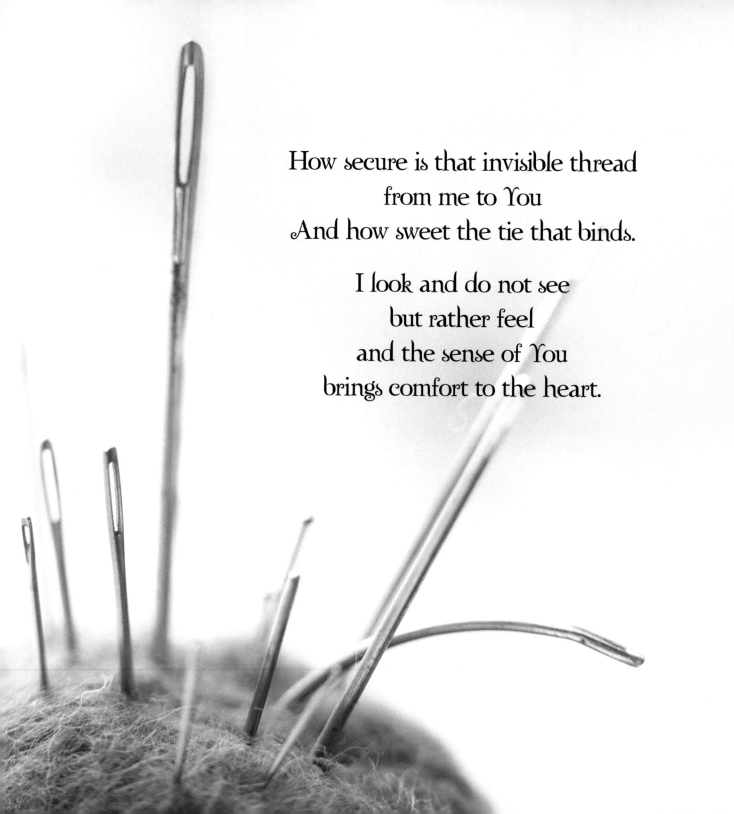

How secure is that invisible thread
from me to You
And how sweet the tie that binds.

I look and do not see
but rather feel
and the sense of You
brings comfort to the heart.

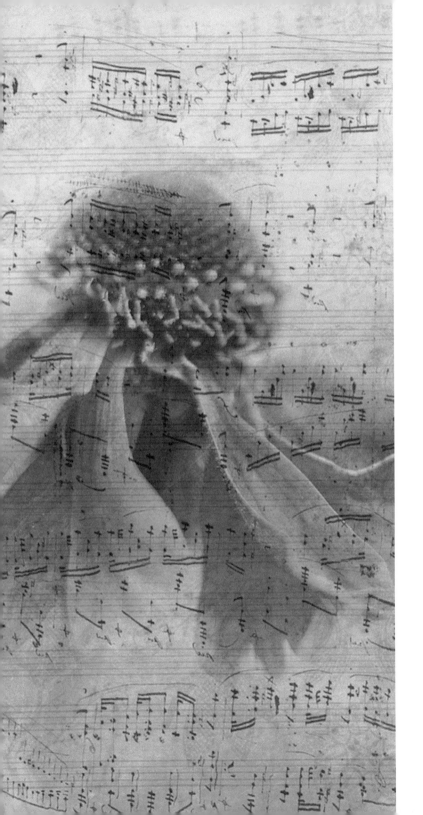

On the brink
of dreams
I find myself
on the verge
of paradise.
Quietly, so silently
I pursue this
gentle melody
within.

This Voice

Thank you God, for your healing hand
bless you for a day without suffering
Grant this peace at all times
and let me know peace in my troubles
Thank you Lord,
that you have secured these boundaries.
Grant that we may know always the security
of your endless power
and everlasting love.
Go on in your way;
your light shines brighter still.
Each day is brighter still,
till the full light of day.

Let your feet run to do good,
and your path be right.
Hear the voice within you
saying "Walk this way."
Here is a voice you can trust.
Only seek it
discern it
capture it
nurture and foster it
amplify it
and tune to it always
And this voice will be your guide
and encouragement
This voice will lead you
in the way everlasting.

Stony Brook
2007

Ventricular Buttons

Lord today your joy has overtaken my heart
inexplicably
And it seems I have only to press some inner
ventricular button
And liquid substance of Happiness
flows from my heart.
What is this ambrosia that flows
this nectar of the Spirit?
And how can I indeed learn
to press this button
at will and as needed?
My heart seems now a fountain
given a squeeze, it gushes
and all the world looks different.
Can our heart's chemistry
be subject to our deliberate whim?
Can well-being come from a mental touch
upon heartstrings strung and tuned
in some ancient chamber
unseen
an instrument set upon a pedestal
awaiting only the Master's touch?
Indeed at this moment, it seems so.

My son, so much trial in a life
can take its toll.
You can rest in the knowledge
that the strings of your heart
are tuned to a perfect pitch
always at the ready
to ring true.
Make a habit of this
and you will find satisfaction
unlimited
through all your days.

6/17/06
Stony Brook

My soul is at peace
and life is good
this moment at least
Uncomplicated and unfettered.

It Seems Somehow Grand

Your path is secure
your way is straight
and your light is lit now.
The music of your activities
is the music of heaven
filled with ideals
and noble sentiments.
Were all humanity to collaborate
according to those ideals
would not this world
see singing
and hear the bird's song.

The light is in the leaves
even when the rain is pouring
The song is in the trees
though the storm's approaching.
How full of life
just outside my window
How full is life
just inside my heart.
I have walked through raindrops
felt the chill wet on my toes
and it seems somehow grand
and simple.

The boats in the harbor
rest quietly
awaiting another day
when sunshine pours down
in a drenching cascade
Instead of these droplets
gathering on sidewalks and curbs
in puddles
that threaten only to engulf my soles.
yet still I sidestep them
and my soul is safe
in the knowledge of You.

My soul sings. It is Sunday
a day apart
and no demand can draw me out
without my consent.
I would that each day
could bring such peace
I would that every activity
Could bring such solemn reward.
In the depth of my heart and belly
I am satisfied.

On the brink of dreams
I find myself
on the verge
of paradise.
Quietly, so silently
I pursue this gentle melody
within.

When this moment in time shall pass
I will yearn for it again
longing for a return
of the restfulness within.
How warm is the touch of my wife
on my neck
And warm is the cup of chai
on the table before me
as the ink runs onto the page
then dries.
The spice of this life
the warmth of another soul
beside me
Let all the rivers of concern
run in channels
in another land
While gently, sweetly
run the waters of gratitude.

Let me have more time in this sentiment
Let me give more time
to this emotion
Sweet, pliant subtle gratitude
that here is one moment at least
of sweet release
I let go the reins of my soul
and allow my soul to have its head
To take me where it will
as the goodness of God
will lead.
My soul is at peace
and life is good
this moment at least
Uncomplicated and unfettered
May I resurrect this state
whenever I seek my God
and find this solace
in each word, and each letter.

4/15/07
Stony Brook

Let all the rivers of concern
run in channels
in another land
While gently, sweetly
run the waters
of gratitude.

I promise you sweet moments of laughter
so deep you have not known it
since early days of childhood,
When the knowledge of good and evil
existed only as a lesson
taught by parents
in a book which remained
on the highest shelf.

There is a song within you
which will yet sing.

You can rest in the knowledge
that the strings of your heart
are tuned to a perfect pitch
always at the ready
to ring true.

Make a habit
of this
and you will
find satisfaction
unlimited
through all
your days.

Hope

Welcome

Choose Hope. Above all else, write of
Hope, and she will catch you unawares,
like morning light cascading
inevitably across the eastern windowsill,
through no effort of your own.

"In every winter's heart there is a quivering spring, and behind the veil is a smiling dawn"
—Gibran

Hope, as defined, must know the depths, to gain the sense that there will be something better. From anguish is born release, and through release, Joy. Anguish is heavy, pregnant with release. The vision of, the sense of, that release we all have known, because the blackest of despair cannot remain. It is always overthrown. This too is inevitable. The least of things – a scent, a kind word, a letter of gratitude, unbinds that force within us, and catches us quite by surprise. We call it

Hope

in the canopy of the heavens,
find eternal freedom to soar.

Let your anxious heart
and thought take flight,
and in the canopy of
the heavens
find eternal freedom to soar.

You are that cloud
sailing over all things,
comprised of moisture,
mingling with so many others,
until the rain pours down,
bringing health to the earth.
Allow the rain to fall
fresh and pure
from heavens,
and water the earth
with your words.

Here now, in your spirit,
is our heavenly habitation.
pure white clouds,
bumping with the others
of purest composition
become one,
traveling on the winds of eternity.
Squeeze out the excess
into showers of blessing
upon the earth.
The gardens of this earth
receive of your spirit
and grow.

Pour out your waters.
Let them rain.

Your wings are strong
and the air runs high and deep.

If I might fly
To your leafy bower
Feel the solid branch
In my talons,
Know, intuitively,
That this branch
Holds to that one
Larger and more secure.

Let me know the sinews of life
That connect
Leaf to stem, to branch
to trunk, to roots
planted firmly in the soil
of planet earth,
created for our sustenance.

Take flight with me now
to the upper reaches
and see this world
from its planetary axis.
See, the horizon beckons
and rosy-fingered dawn approaches.
Our flock is aloft now,
and you rise with them,
on this freshening air.

Your wings are strong
and the air runs high and deep
Take this current now
and feel the pleasure in it.
Our flock cries out
to a distant land
our heaven, and our home.

Do you not feel
the years yet to be?
the strength in potential?

Tomorrow lies at the horizon
and while the curve of this earth
may hide the path
beyond that next bend
Yet you know that path leads on
to heavenly realm.
And many a pilgrim has trod
this way before you.

Take comfort now
and sing within your soul
along with me

Sing Within Your Soul.

THE
POWER OF
HOPE

Sing in these hearts
spirit of the everlasting.
Launch your song
into the ether of this planet
from this little place,
that your presence
might be glorified.
Sing, and make your song
the theme of this territory
and the testimony
of these grounds.

Let the glory notes
of your breezes blow.
Let the soil resound.
Let the turves sing your praises,
a song of songs,
up from the earth's core,
sent to the skies
and the billowing clouds.

Let it ring true
the song of the earth
in harmony
with its maker.

I will take
the vision of heaven
glimmering just below
the horizons of
perception
and let it arise,
glowing.

REJOICE in the Storm

Let me rejoice in the storm,
shout "Hallelujah!"
in the teeth of the gale,
Sing "Glory!" when the splash
of waves careening madly
about my feet
and over my head
soaks me to the skin
and depth of my being.

I promise you sweet moments
Of laughter so deep
You have not known it
Since early days of childhood...

...this has been
PLEASANT
to my SOUL

I have seen the herons
both in the sparkling light
of morning
at the bay
as the gulls laughed,
And in the evening's rosy glow
of setting day.

I have seen the moon
at its full,
bright through
the silhouetted branches
and leaves of the evening trees,
And this has been pleasant
to my soul.

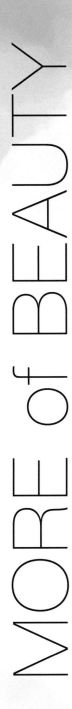

MORE of BEAUTY

The sharp edges of this world
cut like shards of glass
on my consciousness.
I seek some means
to soften the edges,
That my thoughts might be
sweet to me
sweet to you.

There are delicate flowers
and elephant-ear leaves
under radiant rosy
late-afternoon light
to be called up
from the treasure chest of memory.
There are images of
diamond-strewn harbors
brushed by the cool breezes
at end of the day,
Yet I choose the losses
that make me bleed.

Enough! I will see
more of beauty
and less of the beastly.
I will call up heaven
though hell's gates
open wide
calling.
Entice me
with the sweet cooling love-songs
that bless the angels' hearts
and fill their wings
to make them fly.
And I will fly.

My heart seems now a fountain

Can our heart's chemistry
be subject to our deliberate whim?
Can well-being come from a mental touch
upon heartstrings strung and tuned
in some ancient chamber, unseen,
an instrument set upon a pedestal
awaiting only the Master's touch?
Indeed at this moment, it seems so.
What is this ambrosia that flows
this nectar of the Spirit?
And how can I indeed learn
to press this button
at will and as needed?
My heart seems now a fountain;
given a squeeze, it gushes
and all the world looks different.

Spring once again will begin its inevitable march across this planet to warm a heart turned bitter cold

When your heart has been tried
once again
by the season's turning,
Spring once again
will begin its inevitable march
across this planet
to warm a heart turned bitter cold
under the icy blast.

The leaves will green once again
with the lengthening days,
Will spread
to cool now
and shade
against the excesses
of the sun.

All thing are possible.
Our destiny and
purpose await.

We are two, you and I,
of the soil, and divine.

Each day the combative pull
of two separate worlds
begins anew.
I am of the ground, of dust,
and filled with the light, of life.

The soil calls to me
a song of mountains
and craggy rock,
the roughened surface
of schist, and granite,
a childhood clambor
over a face of stone.

The heavens beckon
with clouds of white
and open skies of blue,

the colors of innocence
a dream of some
other place
where we all belong,
lit from beyond,
fringed and infused with light.

We are two, you and I,
both of the soil, and divine,
on the road to a horizon
alight with morning's glow

Breaks now the dawn
with wonder,
and all things are possible.

Our destiny and purpose await.

"Working in our digital culture, where rapid text and images are always inextricably tied, I recently began work on this series, where every page included imagery. In this milieu, words and images must elicit complementary emotional responses. It requires brutal editing, down to the very core and substance of originally lengthy works, until only the juice remains. The response has been unfailingly encouraging."

The author is uniquely suited to present the beauty of nature in writings and images, with sensitivities refined by education in landscape architecture. This book is now available in E-book and print form on Amazon.

Grow now, in this soil.
Spread your roots,
draw nourishment up
from the soil about you.
Drink deep,
then spread your branches to the light.
Soak up the goodly rays of heavenly sun.

Within you is the key to heaven.

Printed in the United States
By Bookmasters